TRIADS
FOR THE
ROCK GUITARIST

A COMPLETE GUIDE TO UNDERSTANDING AND
USING TRIADS FOR RHYTHM AND LEAD GUITAR

BY DAVE CELENTANO

To access audio visit:
www.halleonard.com/mylibrary

Enter Code
7748-3296-8823-8279

ISBN 978-1-57424-328-4
SAN 683-8022

Photo Credit Alison Hasbach

Cover by James Creative Group

Copyright © 2016 CENTERSTREAM Publishing, LLC
P.O. Box 17878 - Anaheim Hills, CA 92817

www.centerstream-usa.com

Illustration Credit Marc Rainer

Table of Contents

Introduction

Triads are used in many styles of music including reggae, rock, blues, ska, jazz, and classical. The intros for *"Roxanne," "Runnin' with the Devil,"* and *"Island in the Sun"* by the Police, Van Halen, and Weezer respectively are great examples of triads in action. Additionally, Edward Van Halen used his tapping technique with triads at the end of "Eruption." Classical composer Johann Sebastian Bach used triads in many of his compositions including the masterpiece *"Toccata and Fugue"* in D minor. The ending of The Eagles *"Hotel California"* is a fine example of harmony guitars using triads. Reggae and ska styles rely heavily on triads for rhythm work in their respective genres. Triad applications are limitless.

About the Author

Dave Celentano is a freelance guitarist, music transcriptionist, composer, author, and educator. After graduating from G.I.T at Musician's Institute, he began teaching private lessons and writing and creating educational guitar books, videos, and DVDs for Centerstream Publications, Hal Leonard Corp., Star Licks, Music Sales, and Cherry Lane Music. Since then, Dave has built a successful business teaching private guitar lessons, developed a series of online guitar courses and workshops for TrueFire.com, teaches songs and stylistic lessons for GuitarTricks.com, and has lessons on GuitarInstructor.com

As a performing musician Dave has several solo CDs: *"Guitar Stew"*, *"Wicked Music Box"*, and *"Desert Storm"*, and plays in the band Soul Core and on their recent CD "A New Day". All of Dave's music can be heard and purchased on iTunes, CDBaby.com, Spotify, iHeart Radio, and Amazon.com.

Check out www.davecelentano.com for all of Dave's educational products and music, and visit him on YouTube and Facebook.

Acknowledgements

Thanks to Ron Middlebrook for his patience with me completing this book, my wife Nicole, Colleen Spears for her editing chops, and the awesome teachers and mentors in my life.

Dave uses D'Addario strings because he wants the best.

– *Dave Celentano*

Tuning Notes

Refer to the downloadable audio for tuning notes.

I - Introduction To Triads

What is a triad?

A triad is a three-note chord constructed of alternating notes from a seven-note scale. Specifically, a triad uses every other note: the root (also called "1"), 3rd, and 5th degrees from the scale. Four triad types can be derived from the various diatonic scales and modes: major, minor, diminished, and augmented. Depending on the scale, all or a few of the various triad types are used.

Four triad types and formulas

Diagramed below are the four different triad types using "C" as a reference root note for easy comparing. The first note (lowest) is considered the root "1" and acts as the foundation for the chord. The middle note is the "3rd" (three scale tones up from the root) and defines whether the chord is major or minor, with minor represented by a flat sign "b" in front: "b3". The highest note is the "5th" (five scale tones up from the root), which can also be flatted for diminished ("b" in front: "b5", also sometimes referred to as "#4") or sharped for augmented ("#" in front: "#5", also sometimes referred to as "b6").

There are two ways to understand and view a triad. First, arrange the three notes ascending on one string: "1(root) - 3 – 5". This method helps to visualize the interval structure (the distance between each note). The second is to arrange the notes on three adjacent strings with one note per string to form a chord grip, which allows the ear to hear the three notes together. Diagrammed below are the four triad qualities arranged using these two methods. Play the chord that occurs on the fourth beat of each bar to hear the sound difference between the four varieties. Major sounds happy and uplifting, minor is sad and somber, diminished sounds unresolved and scary, and augmented is unresolved and open. The four examples below use "C" as the root note for easy comparing between the triad types.

C major triad (1-3-5): The distance between "1 and 3" is two whole steps, and one and a half steps between "3 and 5."

Example 1
C major triad

C minor triad (1-b3-5): The distance between "1 and b3" is one and a half steps, and two whole steps between "b3 and 5."

Example 2
C minor triad

Standard tuning

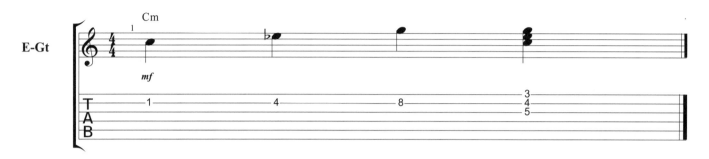

C diminished triad (1-b3-b5): The distance between "1 and b3" is one and a half steps, and one and a half steps between "b3 and b5."

Example 3
C diminished triad

Standard tuning

C augmented triad (1-3-#5): The distance between "1 and 3" is two whole steps and two whole steps between "3 and #5."

Example 4
C augmented triad

Standard tuning

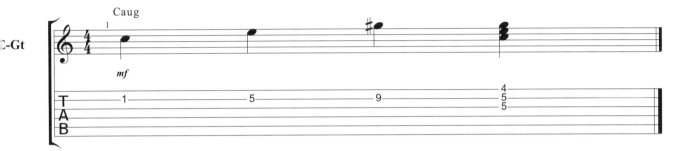

Building major scale diatonic triads

All seven-note diatonic scales contain a series of seven triads - one built from each note. To begin, let's take a look at the C major scale and its component notes, "C-D-E-F-G-A-B." Build the first triad in C major starting with "C" and take every other note (three total). The resulting notes are C, E, and G (1-3-5), which spell a C major chord. For the second triad in C major begin with "D" and repeat alternating notes. The resulting notes are D, F, and A (1-b3-5) which spells a D minor chord. Repeat this for all notes to discover the seven diatonic triads in C major.

Helpful hint: Extend the C major scale one additional octave to see the notes for F, G, A, and B triads.

 C major scale in two octaves: C-D-E-F-G-A-B-C-D-E-F-G-A-B-C

Get familiar with the diatonic triads in C major by playing them in ascending and descending order. Here are the diatonic triads in C major on the top three strings.

Example 5
C major diatonic triads

Standard tuning

Diatonic triads in natural minor, melodic minor, and harmonic minor scales

Use the same process to discover the triads in natural minor, melodic minor, and harmonic minor scales. Below are examples on the top three strings for the diatonic triads in these three minor scales.

C natural minor contains the notes C-D-Eb-F-G-Ab-Bb-C. Below are the diatonic triads in C natural minor.

Example 6
C natural minor diatonic triads

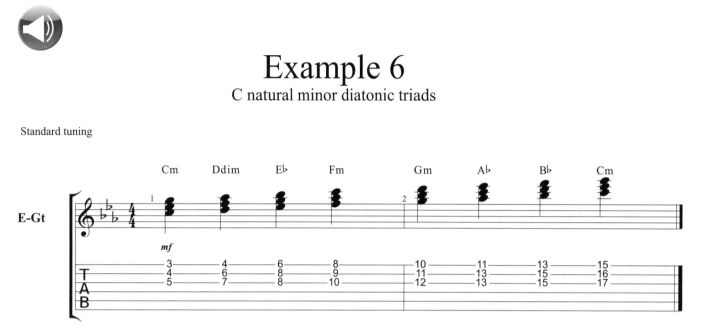

C melodic minor contains the notes C-D-Eb-F-G-A-B-C. Below are the diatonic triads in C melodic minor.

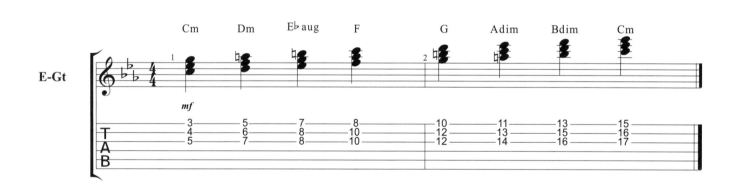

Example 7
C melodic minor diatonic triads

8

C harmonic minor contains the notes C-D-Eb-F-G-Ab-B-C. Below are the diatonic triads in C harmonic minor.

Example 8
C harmonic minor diatonic triads

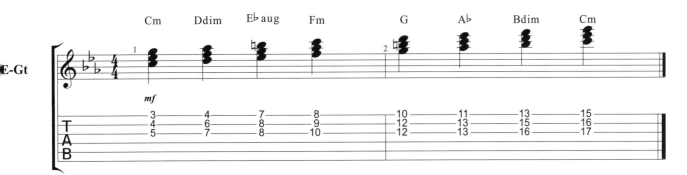

II - Triad Inversions

Triad inversions on string sets 1-2-3, 2-3-4, 3-4-5, and 4-5-6

If the triad's 1st note is in the bass, it is referred to as the root position. With the 3rd or 5th in the bass, the term "inversion" is used. There are two possible inversions: the 1st inversion features the 3rd in the bass and the root moves to the top position, and the 2nd inversion has the 5th in the bass and the 3rd on top.

Below are several neck diagrams showing major, minor, diminished, and augmented triads and subsequent inversions on every set of three adjacent strings. Get familiar with these triad shapes by playing them in order up and down the neck. Although it's important to know and recognize triads on the entire fretboard, this book focuses on triads on the top four strings. Your job is to apply the exercises below to the lower sets of strings.

VERY IMPORTANT: The root note location must be memorized for every triad and inversion shape!

Major, minor, diminished, and augmented triads and inversions on strings "1-2-3."

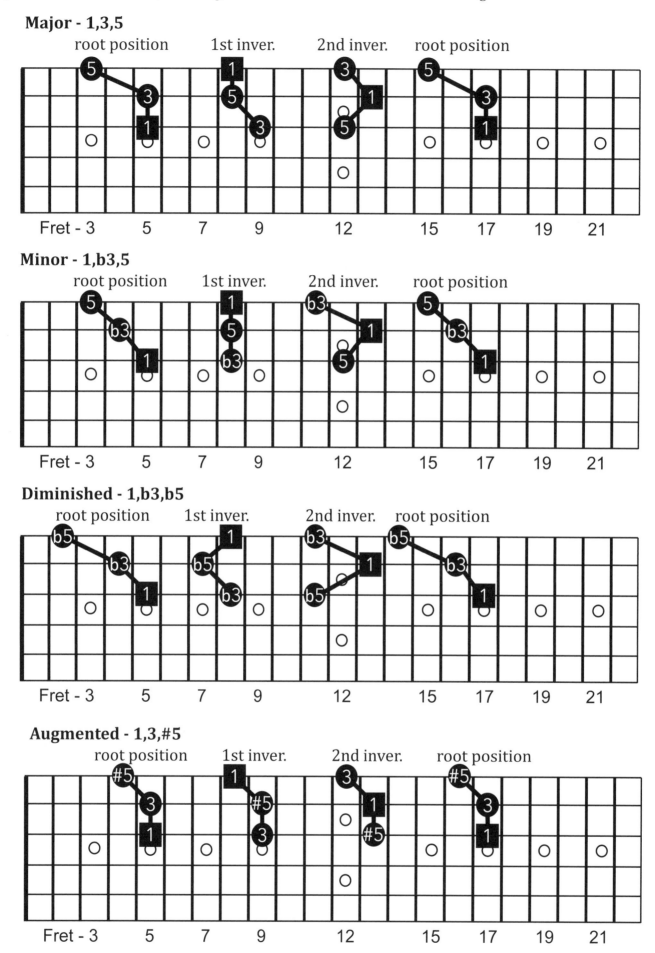

Major, minor, diminished, and augmented triads and inversions on strings "2-3-4."

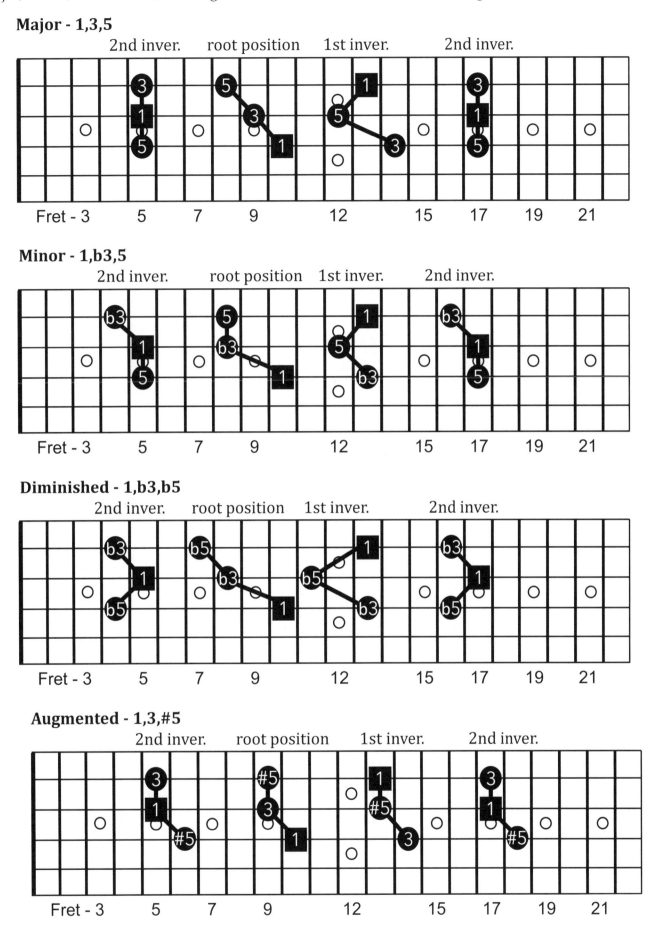

Major - 1,3,5

Minor - 1,b3,5

Diminished - 1,b3,b5

Augmented - 1,3,#5

Major, minor, diminished, and augmented triads and inversions on strings "3-4-5."

Major - 1,3,5

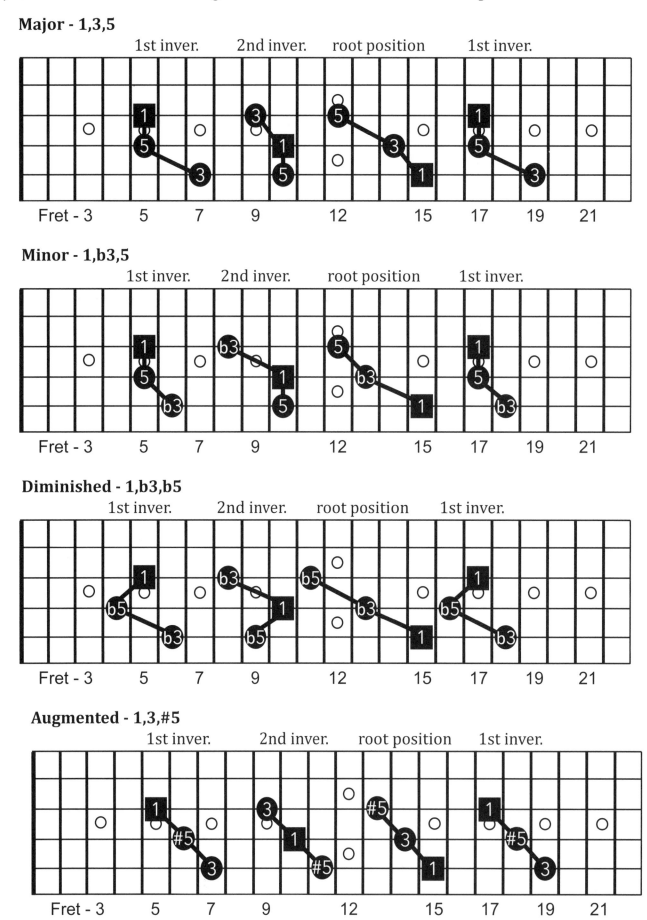

Minor - 1,b3,5

Diminished - 1,b3,b5

Augmented - 1,3,#5

Major, minor, diminished, and augmented triads and inversions on strings "4-5-6."

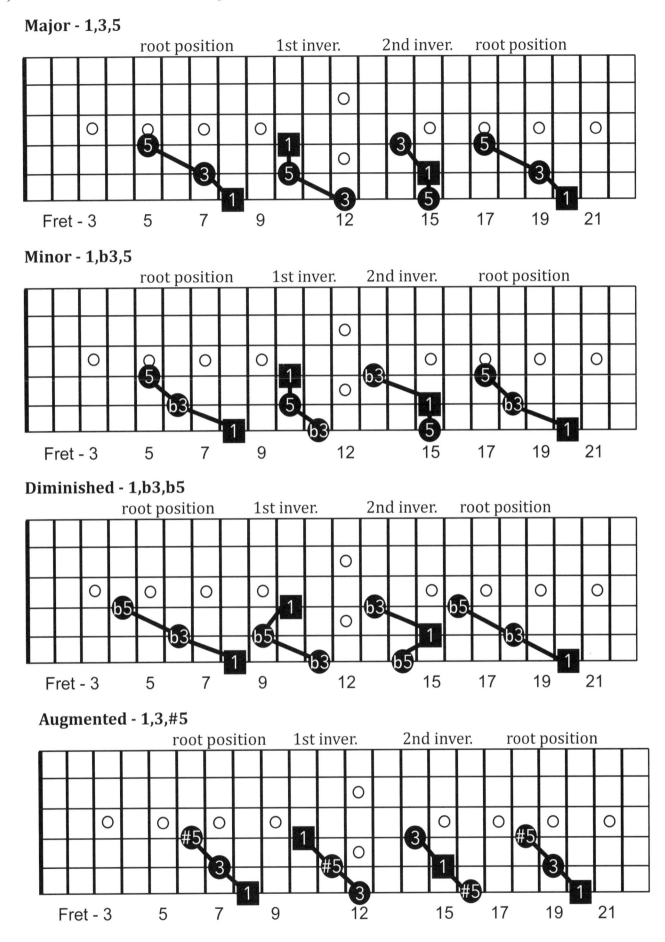

Practicality of using triad inversions to economize hand motion

In the example below the root position triad shape remains the same for all chords, but the fretting hand has to move up and down the fret-board to access each chord.

Example 13

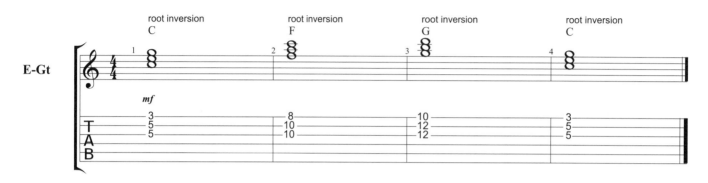

Now check out an efficient way to play the same chords as in Example 13, but using root position, 1st, and 2nd inversions. Notice the close proximity of the triads and the minimal fret-hand movement. Plus it sounds more interesting than the previous example.

Example 14

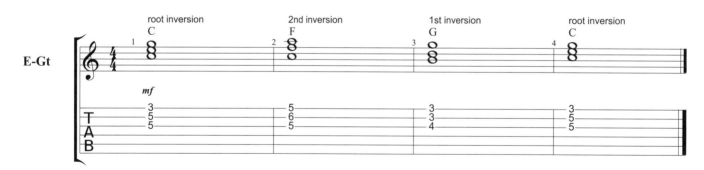

Here's a great exercise working the same chords as above through all of the inversions. Notice each 4-bar cycle of the chord progression resides in a different territory on the fret-board. Triads and inversions can be used to create second guitar parts in songs. Try this cool harmony idea with two guitarists: Have one guitarist play the first four measures while the second simultaneously plays the next four and then the final four measures. It's a simple harmony and it sounds pretty cool!

Example 15

Triad and inversion exercises using two and three chords

Now let's expand on connecting triads and inversions using the shapes on strings 1-2-3 and 2-3-4. The first two examples follow G minor and C chords moving up the fretboard, then D and G minor to resolve. Try a cool keyboard effect with these two examples by plucking the strings staccato style with your index, middle, and ring fingers. Memorizing the location of the root note is a must!

In the example below the first and second measure is 1st inversion G minor and root position C, the third and fourth is 2nd inversion G minor and 1st inversion C, the fifth and sixth is root position G minor, 2nd inversion C and D, and the seventh is root position G minor on strings 1-2-3.

Example 16

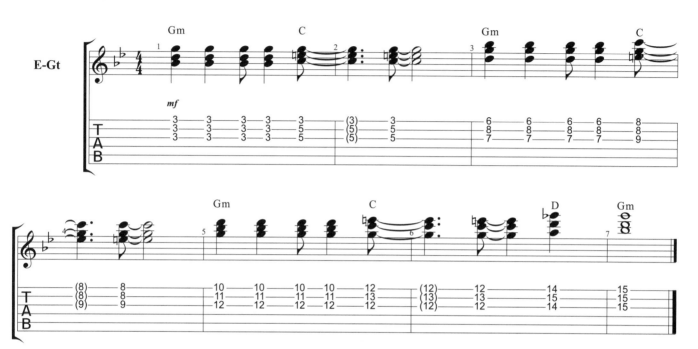

On strings 2-3-4 the first and second measure is root position G minor and 2nd inversion C, the third and fourth is 1st inversion G minor and root position C, the fifth and sixth is 2nd inversion G minor and 1st inversion C and D, and the seventh is root position G minor.

Example 17

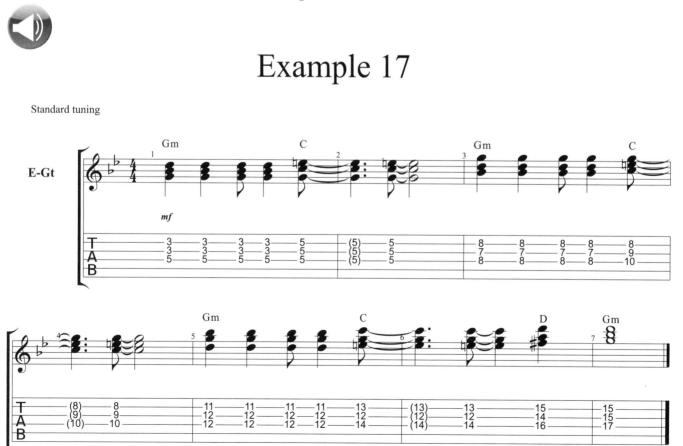

In the same manner as above discover and name triad positions and inversions in the next four examples. The next two examples follow G and A chords moving up the fret-board before resolving on D. Use the root note in each triad shape to quickly locate the proper position for each.

Example 18

Standard tuning

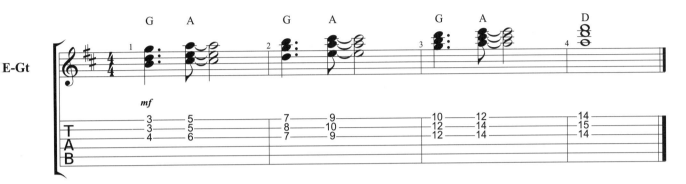

Example 19

Standard tuning

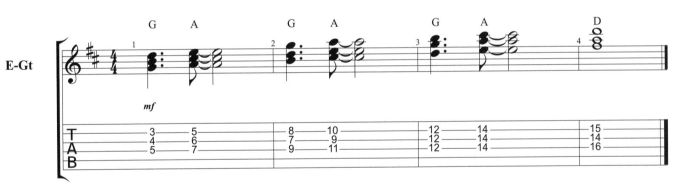

The final two examples follow G-C-D-G chords and strum all down strokes using a pick. Another option is to use staccato technique by plucking the strings with the fingers.

Example 20

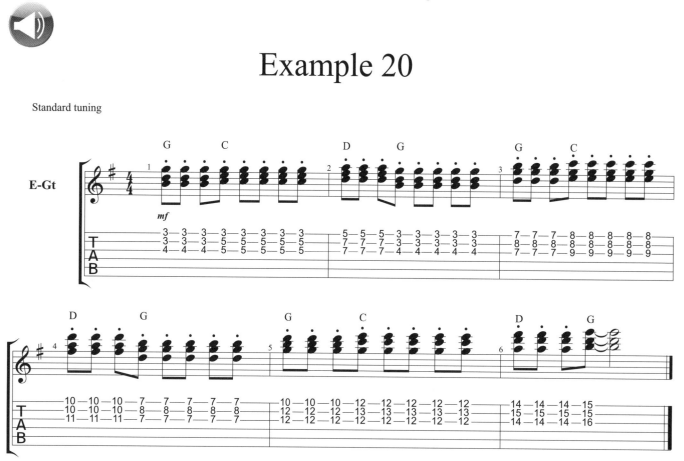

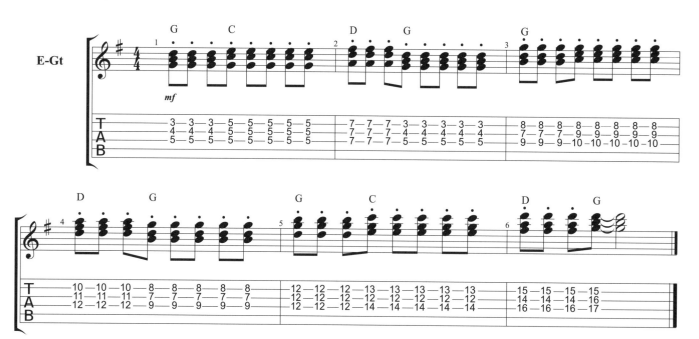

Example 21

III – Rhythm work with triads in various styles

Strumming triads

Here's a common strum pattern using major triads. Focus on strumming only the top three strings and avoid hitting the three in the bass. This example sounds great played over a second guitar strumming the same chords in open position.

Example 22

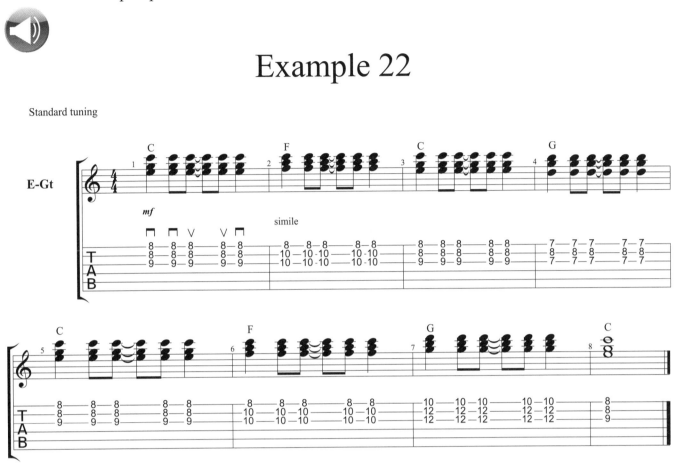

"Pachelbel's Canon" with triads

Traditionally *"Pachelbel's Canon"* is in D major, but this variation is in C major. The chord progression (or parts of it) has been "borrowed" in modern times by songwriters and bands including The Cars in *"Just What I Needed"* (first four chords of the verse in E major) and a more obvious paraphrasing in Green Day's *"Basket Case"* (the verse section in E major).

This example picks the major and minor triad notes individually rather than strumming. Follow the picking directions given in the tablature or experiment to come up with a different pattern of your own. Practice this slowly at first, focusing on switching chords quickly without breaking the beat. Additionally, look for a common finger that can stay on a particular string when transitioning from chord to chord. For instance, the first two chords, "C" and "G," include the third finger (ring finger) on the B string: shift the 13th fret (C triad) to the 12th fret (G triad).

Example 23

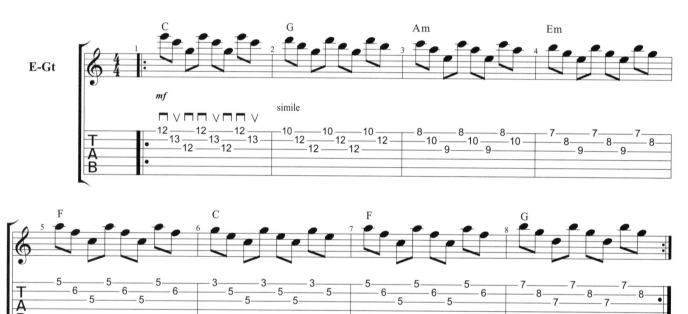

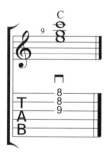

Reggae style and muting strings

A defining characteristic of reggae is percussive string muting performed by the guitarist, usually in conjunction with triads. To replicate the percussive string muting, begin by gripping the triad. Next, while still holding the triad, release finger pressure from the fretboard while maintaining finger contact with the strings. Strumming the strings at this point should make a percussive scratch. Practice this technique with the reggae-influenced exercise below, which happens to use all four triad types: major, minor, diminished, and augmented.

Example 24

Standard tuning

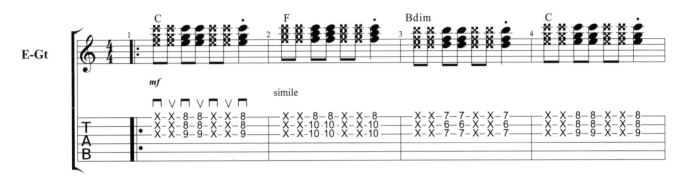

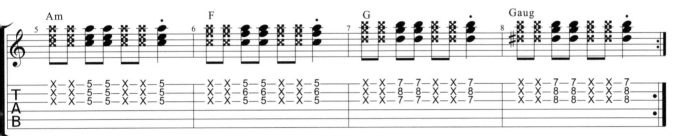

Triads on four strings

The next example explores triads on the top four strings. The highest note on the first string is duplicated one octave lower on the fourth string for all triads in this example. Check out this concept with the first chord in the example, C major, which is a familiar F chord grip at the eighth fret. This example is reminiscent of '50s doo-wop and uses the time signature 6/8, which compliments the chord progression wonderfully. Play the chords evenly with no pause at the transitions. Be sure to play this slowly enough to not allow pauses at the chord transitions. Speed is a by-product of accuracy!

Example 25

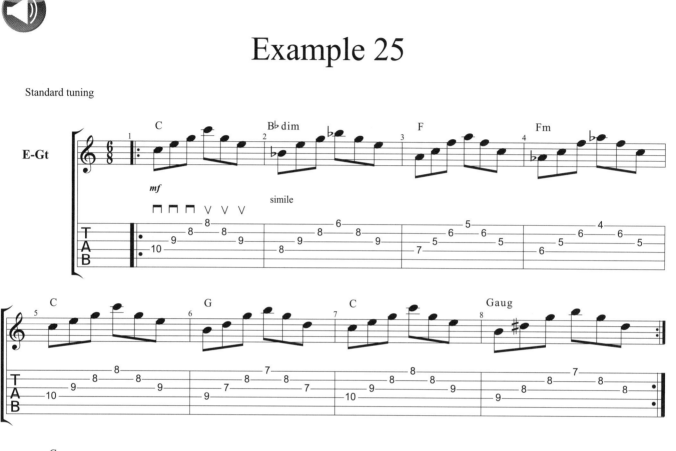

Spanish style using descending and ascending motion

Here's a recognizable Spanish style chord progression that appears in many other genres including surf, rock, and metal, and uses a Spanish strum pattern in 3/4 time. The first half plays second inversion triads descending the fretboard, while the latter half follows the same chords and uses a variety of inversions to ascend the guitar neck. Changing direction to create opposite motion is one of many cool things that can be done with triads. Pretty cool!

Example 26

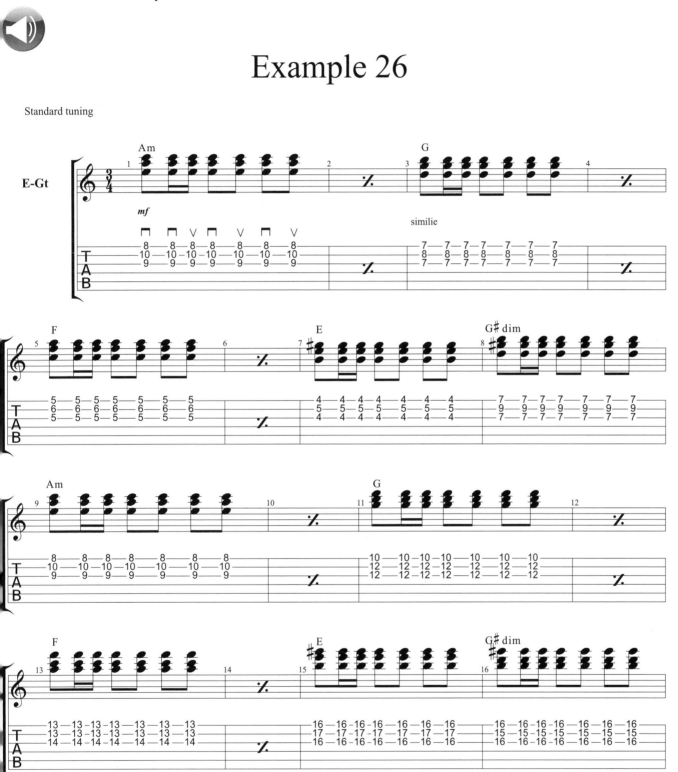

Staccato style plucking triads with fingers

Plucking strings with the fingers produces a staccato effect similar to a keyboard. In the example below, pluck all three strings simultaneously with your index, middle, and ring fingers (no pick here). The tone is reminiscent of The Who's keyboard work on *"Won't Get Fooled Again"* and Van Halen's on *"Little Guitars."* The chord progression in this example is similar to the classical work of Johann Sebastian Bach where the chords are moving in ascending diatonic fourth intervals and cycle through all seven chords in A minor. The only exception is the tension building G# diminished chord which is borrowed from the A harmonic minor scale. Listen to how well G# diminished resolves to the A minor chord.

Example 27

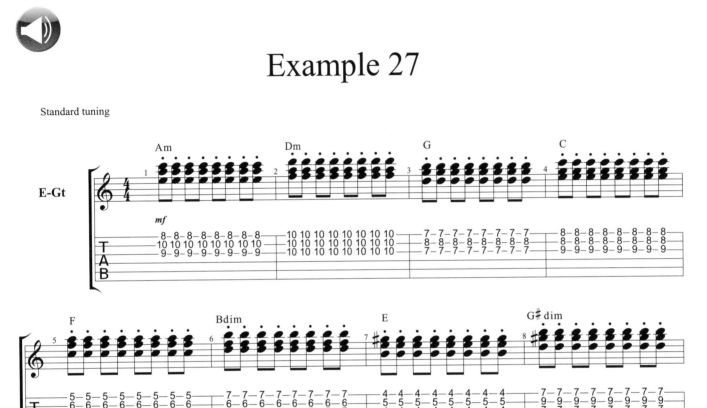

Blues style with triads functioning as chord extensions

In jazz and blues genres triads are occasionally used to create harmony extensions of a chord. For instance an A7 chord is spelled A-C#-E-G, which is an A major triad: A (root), C# (3rd), and E (5th) with a G note (b7) added. Check out the last three notes of A7: C#, E, and G, spelling a C# diminished triad. A second guitar could play a C# diminished triad over the A7 chord and sound completely natural. Let's take this concept further by playing the upper extension triad of an A9 chord, which is spelled A (root), C# (3rd), E (5th), G (b7th), and B (9th). The upper three notes are E, G, and B, and spell an E minor triad. The example below applies this concept to a 12-bar blues in A and uses a typical move where the triads slide back and forth. See if you can recognize the different triads used as extensions for the A9, D9, and E9 chords.

Example 28

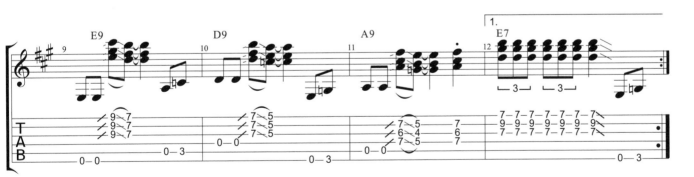

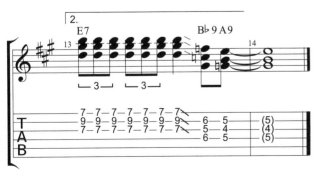

Rolling Stones style "Keith Richards" chords

Many of the Rolling Stones signature guitar riffs use triads. The intro to *"Start Me Up"* and *"Brown Sugar"* are great representations of Keith Richards' triad chords in action. Check out the stylistic example below for a workout using 1st and 2nd inversion major triads on the 2nd, 3rd, and 4th strings.

Example 29

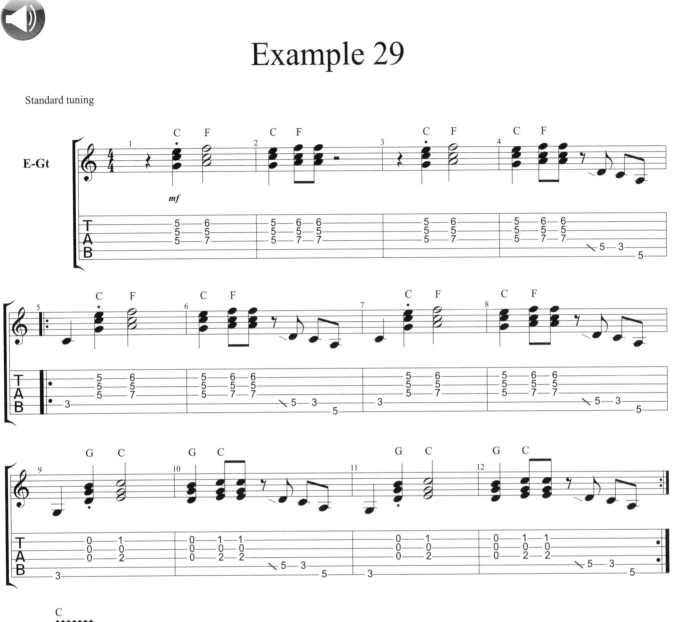

Van Halen style triads

Edward Van Halen is a proponent and heavy user of triads, especially major triads. Many songs in the Van Halen catalog are based on major triads and inversions including *"Runnin' with the Devil," "Unchained," "Dance the Night Away,"* and even the keyboard intro for *"Jump."* Check out the example below for a Van Halen-style triad workout. Hybrid picking is employed here, which uses a combination of pick for low notes and fingers (middle, ring, and pinkie) for the triads. The final few bars are played with the pick and run through all three inversions of "A and B" triads before resolving on "E." See if you can spot the inversions.

Example 30

IV – Arpeggio-style triads

Diatonic triad arpeggios on two strings in C major

Playing triad notes individually in lead guitar fashion is a great way to spice up a guitar solo, plus it gets away from the typical pentatonic licks found in many solos. It's also a fantastic way to follow the chord changes under the solo. The end of The Eagles' "Hotel California" is a great example of triads played arpeggio style while following the chord changes. The term "diatonic" means notes and/or chords derived from a particular key. Refer back to the section "Building major scale diatonic triads" to review this concept. Check out the two examples below showcasing diatonic triads in C major on the top two strings. Bonus exercise: Play each triad four times.

Example 31

Standard tuning

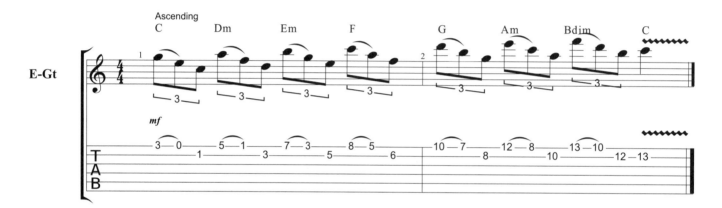

Example 32

Standard tuning

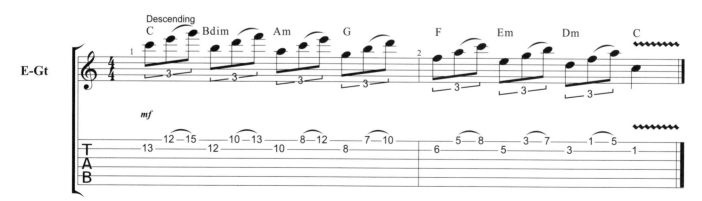

Triads from Bach's "Toccata and Fugue" in D minor

Composer Johann Sebastian Bach used triads in many of his works including the masterpiece *"Toccata and Fugue"* in D minor. Below is an excerpt from the tune featuring descending triads on the top two strings. Listen to my version of *"Toccata and Fugue"* included as a bonus track at the end of the companion audio

Example 33

Standard tuning

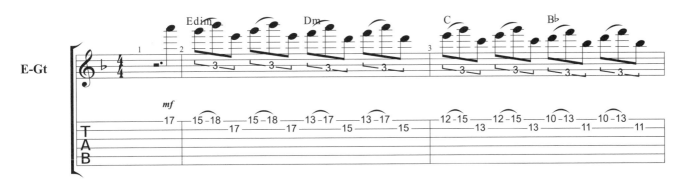

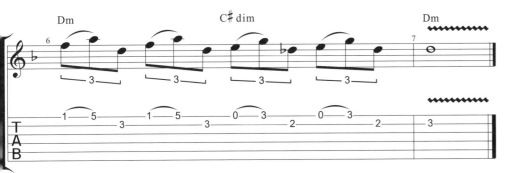

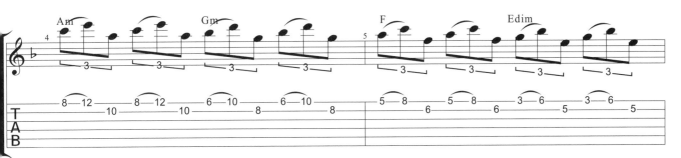

Diatonic triads ascending and descending the C major scale

Here's a fun finger twister playing diatonic triads in C major in one position. Every other triad is played in the opposite direction from the previous while ascending the scale. Not an easy feat to master! The latter half turns around and descends in the same alternating manner. Start out slowly at first and be sure to alternate pick and play evenly without stopping.

Example 34

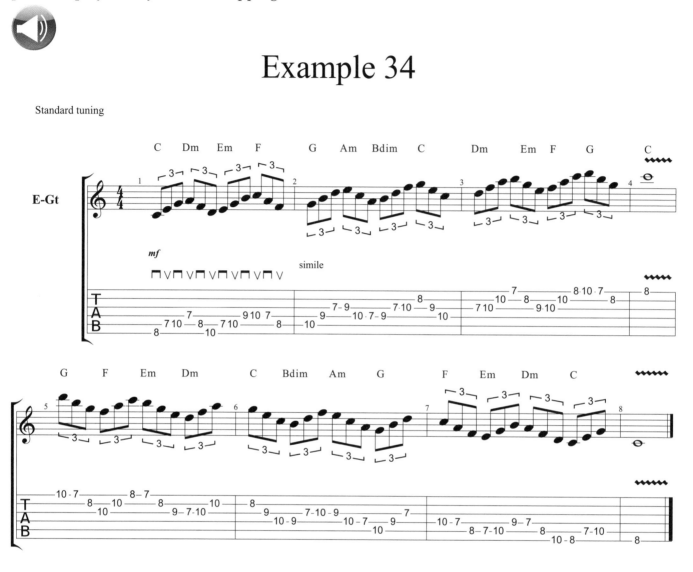

V – Soloing with triads

Easy solo with three-string triad shapes

Soloing with triads can become repetitive and boring if overused. One way to get better mileage is to give them an interesting rhythm. Below is a simple solo using three-string triads that follow the chord change "Am-D". Notice the second half of the solo uses higher inversions of the same chords to create movement and interest.

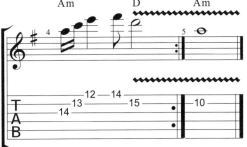

Example 35

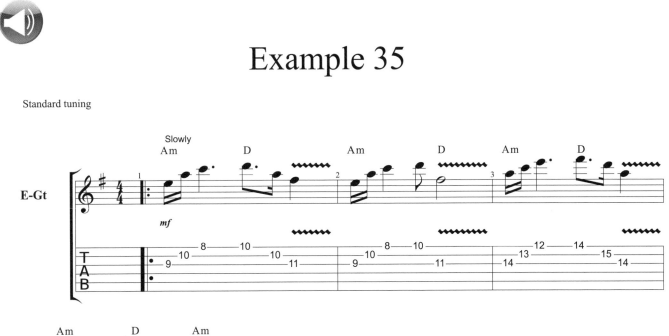

Medium difficulty solo using two-string triad shapes

The next solo is a bit busier than the previous and uses two-string triads and inversions over the same "Am-D" chord pattern. Creating captivating melodies with triads relies on interesting note selection and syncopated rhythm work. Try creating your own solo using triads over the chords "Am-D."

Example 36

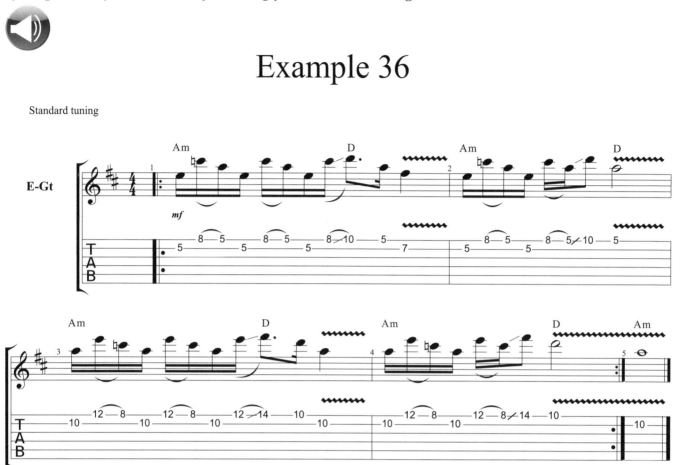

Rapid-fire two-string triads

No fancy rhythm work here, just fast and non-stop 16th notes! Mute the strings slightly by resting the picking hand heel on the strings just past the bridge. The solo outlines Am, F, C, G, and G# diminished chords and uses a repeating three-note sequence played as 16th notes, which creates an interesting feel. Although the lick is repetitious, it has a captivating floating quality over the time signature 4/4. For maximum effect use alternate picking and practice slowly with a metronome. Once mastered at a slow speed, gradually increase the metronome's tempo.

Example 37

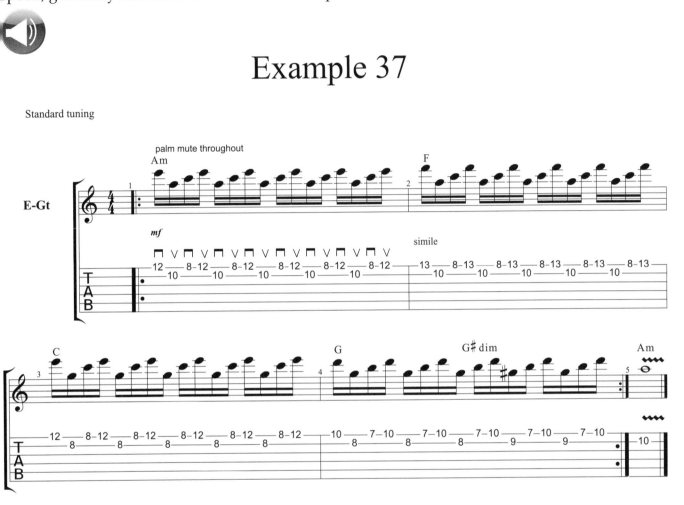

Tapping triads on one string

Tapping and triad arpeggios go together like bread and butter. Here the tapping sequence is quite longer than the previous examples, taking sixteen notes to unfold, and outlines Am-F-C-G chords. Use the picking hand's index finger to tap notes with a "T" written over them and the index and pinkie fingers on the fretting hand for the remaining hammer-on and pull-off notes. Break out the metronome for this one and start out slowly!

Example 38

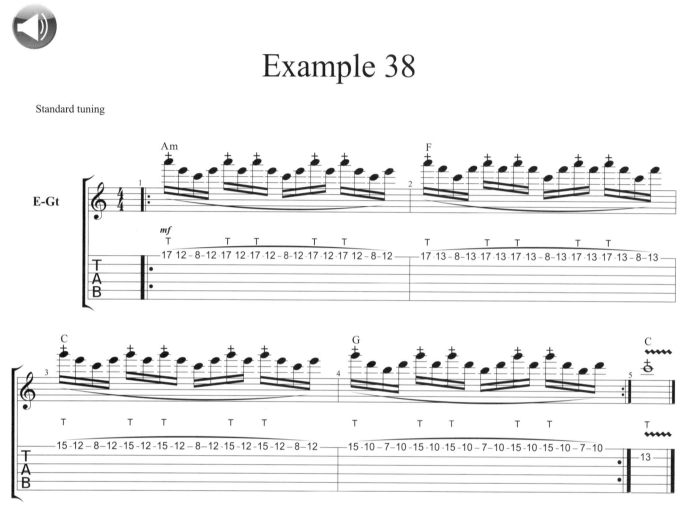

VI – Advanced applications – cool and different ways to use triads

Eric Johnson style expanded triads and inversions

More often than not guitarists play triads with close voicings: "1-3-5," "3-5-1," and "5-1-3." Taking a tip from violinists, Eric Johnson created expanded voicings on guitar by spreading the notes apart: "1-5-3," "3-1-5," and "5-3-1." Johnson can be heard using this concept in his magnum opus "Cliffs of Dover." The idea is fairly easy to reproduce on guitar, but will require string skipping in order to keep each triad in one position. See if you can spot the different inversions used in measures 5-8. Be sure to use strict alternate picking and a metronome!

Example 39

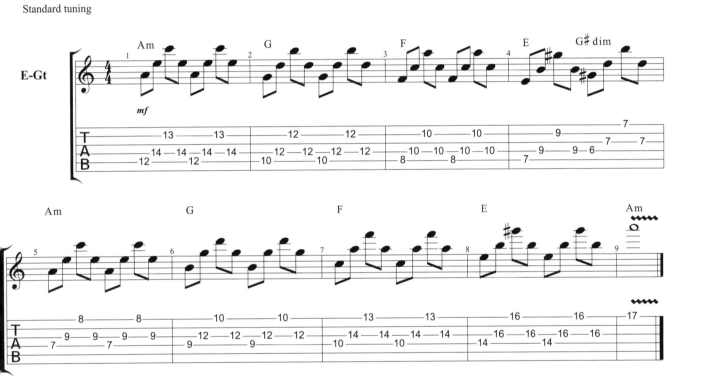

Five-string triads and inversions

This classically inspired triad workout ascends the top five strings in triplets, with each triplet playing a different inversion of the chord. Root position begins on the fifth string and ascends three consecutive strings, the 1st inversion starts on the fourth string and ascends three consecutive strings, the 2nd inversion ascends three strings from the third string, and finally the root position is one octave higher on the top two strings. Play through the first bar and see if you can recognize the A minor triad inversions. The second bar plays a root position D minor triad on the top two strings. The remaining six bars use the same two bar concept applied to "G and C", "F and Bdim," and "E and Am" chords. Follow the alternate picking indications or come up with a consistent picking pattern that works for you.

Example 40

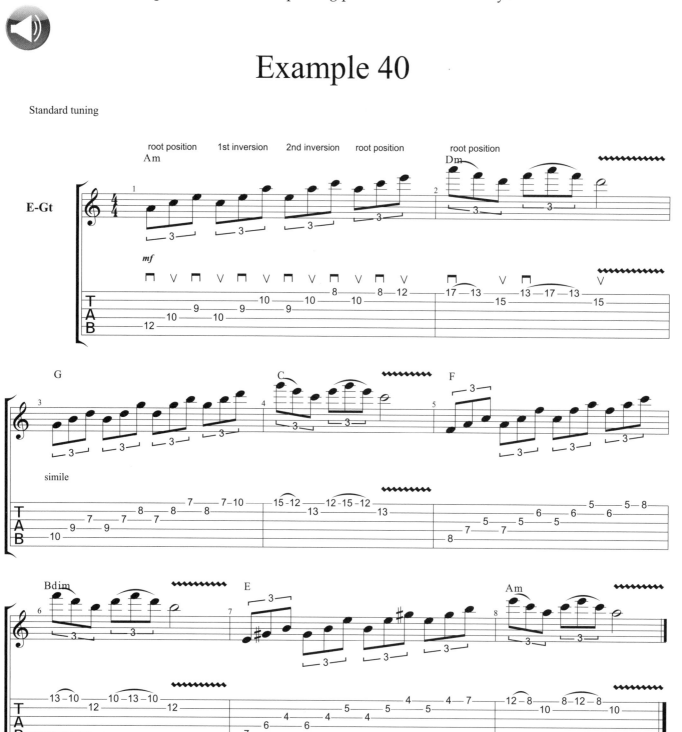

Stacking triads to create jazzy chord extensions

Here's a cool way of creating dense jazz chords by stacking multiple triads. Check out the first measure in this example beginning with an F major root position triad on the two bass strings, followed by an E diminished root position triad on the two middle strings, and finally a C major root position triad on the top two strings. The resulting chord is "F major 11," which contains the notes F (root), A (3rd), C (5th), E (7th), G (9th), and Bb (11th). The remaining three bars use the same concept to outline "D minor 11," "Bb major 9 #11," and "C11" chords respectively. See if you can spot and name the three triads in each of the remaining three chords.

Example 41

Tapping triads on multiple strings

Check out this tapping idea using Eric Johnson's expanded triad concept (detailed a few examples earlier). This example sounds best with a clean tone since you'll want to let the notes sustain as long as possible. Use your pick hand's index and middle fingers to tap the higher portion of the lick (notated with a "T" above the note) – strings "4 and 2" (index and middle respectively) or "3 and 1" (index and middle respectively). The fret hand index and ring fingers hammer-on the remaining notes on the low strings (notated with an "H" above). Listen to my song *"Crystal Castle"* included as a bonus track on the audio accompanying this book (track #41), which features this tapping concept pushed to the limits.

Example 42

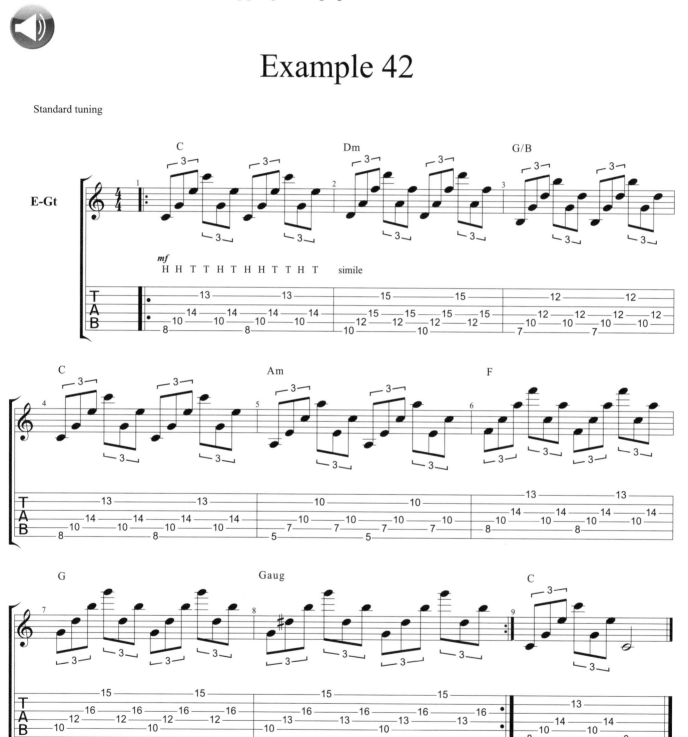

Bonus Audio Tracks

The following two bonus tracks are from my Desert Storm CD, available on iTunes, Spotify, CDBaby.com, iHeart radio, and Amazon.com. The first bonus track (track #43) is my version of Bach's *"Toccata and Fugue"* in D minor and, while it's not using all triads, there are several sections that do. See if you can hear them!

The second bonus track *"Crystal Castle"* (track #44) has an obvious Joe Satriani influence and uses a tapping technique very similar to example #42 from this book.

Conclusion

This book is not intended to be all encompassing by any means, but rather a tool to spark fresh ideas and concepts that will broaden your musicianship and help you to become a better player. We are limited only by our understanding of music and it's fundamentals, so continue to push forward, learn new concepts, and strive to be the best musician you can be. I truly hope the ideas contained here open new doors and possibilities with your guitar playing. Keep those fingers flying!!

For more info on Dave Celentano's educational books, DVDs, online tutorials, and music check out www.davecelentano.com and visit him on YouTube and Facebook.

More Great Guitar Books from Centerstream...

SCALES & MODES IN THE BEGINNING
INCLUDES TAB
by Ron Middlebrook
The most comprehensive and complete scale book written especially for the guitar. Chapers include: Fretboard Visualization • Scale Terminology • Scales and Modes • and a Scale to Chord Guide.
00000010...$11.95

CELTIC CITTERN
by Doc Rossi
Although the cittern has a history spanning 500 years and several countries, like its cousin the Irish bouzouki, it is a relative newcomer to contemporary traditional music. Doc Rossi, a wellknown citternist in both traditional and early music, has created this book for intermediate to advanced players who want to improve their technique, develop ideas and learn new repertoire. Guitarists can play all of the tunes in this book on the guitar by tuning C F C G C F, low to high, and putting a capo at the second fret. The lowest line in the tablature then corresponds to the fifth string. The CD features all the tunes played at a medium tempo.
00001460 Book/CD Pack $19.99

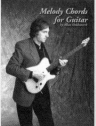

KILLER PENTATONICS FOR GUITAR
INCLUDES TAB
by Dave Celentano
Covers innovative and diverse ways of playing pentatonic scales in blues, rock and heavy metal. The licks and ideas in this book will give you a fresh approach to playing the pentatonic scale, hopefully inspiring you to reach for higher levels in your playing. The 37-minute companion CD features recorded examples.
00000285 Book/CD Pack $19.95

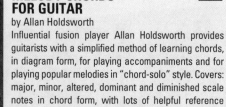

MELODY CHORDS FOR GUITAR
INCLUDES TAB
by Allan Holdsworth
Influential fusion player Allan Holdsworth provides guitarists with a simplified method of learning chords, in diagram form, for playing accompaniments and for playing popular melodies in "chord-solo" style. Covers: major, minor, altered, dominant and diminished scale notes in chord form, with lots of helpful reference tables and diagrams.
00000222...$24.95

PAINLESS ARRANGING FOR OLD-TIME COUNTRY GUITAR
INCLUDES TAB
by Joe Weidlich This book will help readers recognize and remember commonly used note patterns and sequences in fiddle tunes and string band music, to make creating interesting variations easier. Author Joe Weidlich analyzes four traditional favorites – including "The Wreck of the Old '97" – showing how guitarists can substitute notes and patterns, painlessly!
00001353 ....$14.99

COMPLETE RHYTHM GUITAR GUIDE FOR BLUES BANDS
INCLUDES TAB
by Larry McCabe
This info-filled book/CD will take you out of your rhythm-playing rut and teach you to play confidently in any blues style! You'll learn: intros, endings and turnarounds; modern theory for reharmonizing chord progressions; jazz and eight-bar progressions; and much more. The book includes 100 musical examples, 16 theory workshops, a discography and bibliography, and the CD has 51 tracks.
00000333 Book/CD Pack $24.95

GUITAR CHORDS PLUS
INCLUDES TAB
by Ron Middlebrook
A comprehensive study of normal and extended chords, tuning, keys, transposing, capo use, and more. Includes over 500 helpful photos and diagrams, a key to guitar symbols, and a glossary of guitar terms.
00000011...$11.95

THE CHORD SCALE GUIDE
INCLUDES TAB
by Greg Cooper
The Chord Scale Guide will open up new voicings for chords and heighten your awareness of linear harmonization. This will benefit jazz ensemble players, rock guitarists and songwriters looking to create new and unique original music, and understand the harmony behind chords.
00000324...$15.95

IRISH YOU A MERRY CHRISTMAS
by Doug Esmond
This book includes Christmas melodies as well as lesserknown tunes from Scotland paired with seasonal titles. All the songs can be played solo or with other instruments. A CD is included with recordings of the author playing using both steel and nylon string guitars.
00001360 Book/CD Pack...$15.99

MUTING THE GUITAR
INCLUDES TAB
by David Brewster
This book/CD pack teaches guitarists how to effectively mute anything! Author David Brewster covers three types of muting in detail: frethand, pickhand, and both hands. He provides 65 examples in the book, and 70 tracks on the accompanying CD.
00001199 Book/CD Pack...$19.99

P.O. Box 17878 - Anaheim Hills, CA 92817
(714) 779-9390   www.centerstream-usa.com